Building Character
Primary

Save time and energy planning thematic units with this comprehensive resource. We've searched through the 1990–1998 issues of *The Mailbox*® and *Teacher's Helper*® magazines to find the best ideas for you to use when teaching a thematic unit about character building. Included in this book are favorite units from the magazines, single ideas to extend a unit, and a variety of reproducible activities. Pick and choose from these activities to develop your own complete unit or simply to enhance your current lesson plans. You're sure to find everything you need right here in this book to create integrated learning experiences that will truly make a difference for your students.

Editors:
Kimberly Fields
Susan Walker

Artists:
Theresa Lewis Goode, Kimberly Richard,
Donna K. Teal

Cover Artist:
Kimberly Richard

www.themailbox.com

©2000 by THE EDUCATION CENTER, INC.
All rights reserved.
ISBN10 #1-56234-374-2 • ISBN13 #978-156234-374-3

Manufactured in the United States
10 9 8 7 6 5 4

Table of Contents

Thematic Units

More Activities and Ideas

Reproducible Activities

Thematic Units...

CHARACTER BUILDING

from The MAILBOX® magazine.

BUILDING CHARACTER

Compassion. Helpfulness. Perseverance. Respect. Responsibility. The list of key character-building qualities goes on and on—and so does the challenge of teaching these virtues to young children. Use the following character-building activities from our subscribers to help your students learn to care for themselves and others.

HELPFULNESS

Respect Day

Designate a day for your classroom, grade level, or entire school to refine their skills of respect. Start Respect Day with a class meeting or an assembly. Discuss the meaning of respect, have volunteers role-play respectful behavior, and answer students' questions. Then challenge students and staff members to spend the entire day displaying their most respectful behavior. This large-scale, concrete example of respect will encourage students to carry this positive behavior beyond the school walls. You may find that more value days—like Courtesy Day, Cooperation Day, and Kindness Day—are in order!

Debbie Green—Gr. 3, Northwest Heights Elementary School
Durant, OK

COMPASSION

Caring For Others

Nurture compassion in your students with monthly community service projects. Ideas include collecting wish-list items for a local animal shelter, making get-well bags for hospital patients, creating holiday cards or ornaments for a retirement home, collecting needed items for a local shelter, and helping older neighbors with light yard work. Students will experience the joy of giving of themselves and come to realize the benefits of compassion—by both the giver and the receiver.

Diane Benner—Gr. 2, Dover Elementary, Dover, PA

COOPERATION

Terrific Tales

Reinforce a variety of character-building traits with a Terrific Tales board. Title a sheet of poster board "Terrific Tales About _____" and laminate the resulting poster for durability. Display the poster in an easily accessible location. Near the poster, place a pad of self-adhesive notes and a container of pencils. At the start of each week use a wipe-off marker to program the poster with a desired character trait like "Honesty," "Fairness," or "Helpfulness."

After confirming that students understand the meaning of the spotlighted trait, invite them to be on the lookout for examples of it. When a youngster realizes that a classmate has exhibited the featured behavior toward him, he goes to the poster, describes the incident on a self-adhesive note, and signs and attaches the note to the poster. During the week read some of the posted notes aloud. Then, at the end of the week, read each note aloud and present it to the student who demonstrated the featured behavior. To re-program the poster, wipe off and replace the featured trait. Your students' self-esteems are sure to soar!

Valerie Masin—Grs. K–3
District 504
Burwell, NE

Terrific Tales About **Helpfulness**

Samuel helped me find my missing milk money. It was in my coat pocket!

Erica Green

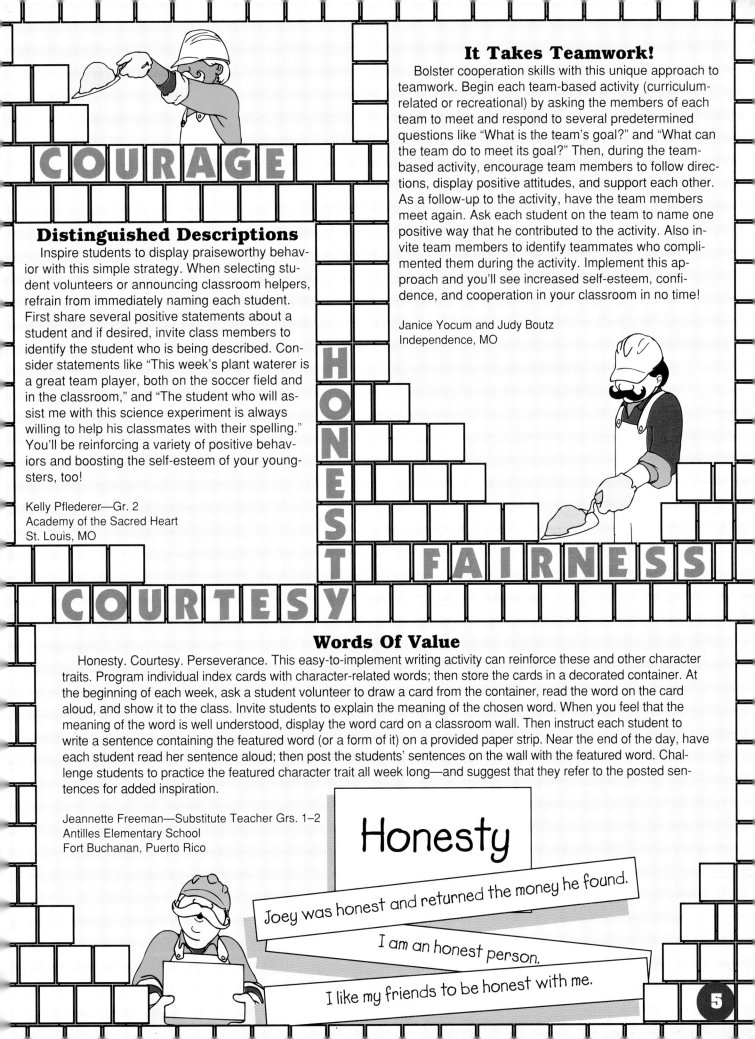

COURAGE

HONESTY

FAIRNESS

COURTESY

Distinguished Descriptions

Inspire students to display praiseworthy behavior with this simple strategy. When selecting student volunteers or announcing classroom helpers, refrain from immediately naming each student. First share several positive statements about a student and if desired, invite class members to identify the student who is being described. Consider statements like "This week's plant waterer is a great team player, both on the soccer field and in the classroom," and "The student who will assist me with this science experiment is always willing to help his classmates with their spelling." You'll be reinforcing a variety of positive behaviors and boosting the self-esteem of your youngsters, too!

Kelly Pflederer—Gr. 2
Academy of the Sacred Heart
St. Louis, MO

It Takes Teamwork!

Bolster cooperation skills with this unique approach to teamwork. Begin each team-based activity (curriculum-related or recreational) by asking the members of each team to meet and respond to several predetermined questions like "What is the team's goal?" and "What can the team do to meet its goal?" Then, during the team-based activity, encourage team members to follow directions, display positive attitudes, and support each other. As a follow-up to the activity, have the team members meet again. Ask each student on the team to name one positive way that he contributed to the activity. Also invite team members to identify teammates who complimented them during the activity. Implement this approach and you'll see increased self-esteem, confidence, and cooperation in your classroom in no time!

Janice Yocum and Judy Boutz
Independence, MO

Words Of Value

Honesty. Courtesy. Perseverance. This easy-to-implement writing activity can reinforce these and other character traits. Program individual index cards with character-related words; then store the cards in a decorated container. At the beginning of each week, ask a student volunteer to draw a card from the container, read the word on the card aloud, and show it to the class. Invite students to explain the meaning of the chosen word. When you feel that the meaning of the word is well understood, display the word card on a classroom wall. Then instruct each student to write a sentence containing the featured word (or a form of it) on a provided paper strip. Near the end of the day, have each student read her sentence aloud; then post the students' sentences on the wall with the featured word. Challenge students to practice the featured character trait all week long—and suggest that they refer to the posted sentences for added inspiration.

Jeannette Freeman—Substitute Teacher Grs. 1–2
Antilles Elementary School
Fort Buchanan, Puerto Rico

Honesty

Joey was honest and returned the money he found.

I am an honest person.

I like my friends to be honest with me.

Storytime Values

★ Keep the ★ promises you make.

★ Treat ★ others ★ fairly.

Play fair. ★

Be responsible. ★★

Characters With Character

Children's literature is an excellent place to find examples of positive character traits. Follow up an oral reading of a favorite picture book or beginning chapter book by asking students to identify the positive values of the main character(s). To create an on-going display, write the student responses on individual cards or cutouts and post them on a bulletin board titled "Storytime Values." Repeat the activity each time you finish an oral reading of a children's book. Periodically review the character traits on display and add a star to each card that features a value that your students feel they consistently portray.

Jackie Hostetler—Gr. 1
Tri-County R-VII Elementary School, Jamesport, MO

CONFIDENCE

Positive Response

Promote student dignity and heighten self-esteem with this positive response strategy. When a student responds incorrectly to a question, instead of pointing out that his answer is wrong, state the question to which the student's answer corresponds. Then provide the correct answer to the original question. For example, if the question asked is "What is the sum of 6 + 7?", and a student replies "14"—respond as follows: "14 is the sum of 7 + 7. That means the sum of 6 + 7 is 13." Since words like "no" and "wrong" are avoided, a student's dignity is preserved and the feeling of being wrong is minimized. This approach is sure to increase student participation. And since students learn by example, you can look forward to hearing your youngsters stating positive responses for incorrect answers, too!

Pat Boswell—Gr. 3, Bonn Elementary School, Germany

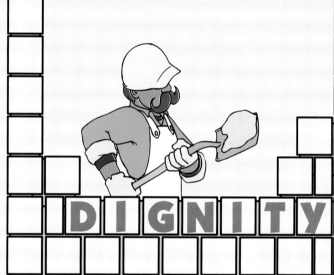

DIGNITY

Roll Call For Respect

Encourage respect among your students with this two-fold tip. When you observe a student showing respect for herself, for others, or for her school or community, award the student with a respect coupon. When a child earns three coupons, invite the student and a special guest to eat their lunches at a designated "Table Of Respect." When a fourth coupon is earned, allow the student to place a personalized cutout on a classroom display titled "Roll Call For Respect." This visual reminder of respectful behavior makes it easy for students and visitors to see that respect is a valued trait in your classroom.

Debbie Green—Gr. 3
Northwest Heights Elementary School
Durant, OK

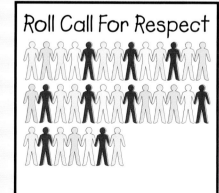

Roll Call For Respect

RESPECT

The Wall Of Fame

Here's an ideal way to recognize your students' good deeds. Title an area of a classroom wall "The Wall Of Fame" and duplicate a supply of induction forms similar to the one shown. When a student observes a classmate performing a good deed like being kind, compassionate, or helpful, he completes and submits to you a copy of the induction form. Post the completed forms, along with snapshots of the inductees, on The Wall Of Fame. As students earn recognition, they will be encouraged to continue their kind behavior.

Adriana Paciocco—Gr. 2
Eagle Elementary School
West Bloomfield, MI

I, Joey Gomez, induct Matthew Taylor into The Wall Of Fame because he asked me to play with him at recess.

I, Lizzy Leon Breyanna Lynne, induct ... the Wall Of Fame becaus... said she was s... I didn't feel we...

RESPONSIBILITY

Rob Mayworth

Hug Day

Hugs, hugs, hugs! What a great way to show someone you care! Have students describe how they feel when they are hugged and when they give hugs. Lead students to understand that hugging is one way to show someone that you care. Then find out other ways your students show their friends and family members that they care about them. To encourage students to show their compassion for others, designate one day a month as Hug Day (or Show You Care Day). On Hug Day display a sign on the classroom door that invites all who enter the room to demonstrate their caring spirit throughout the day. If desired, post a list of appropriate caring gestures like hugs, handshakes, and pats on the back. At the end of the day, invite students to talk about how showing and receiving compassion made them feel. Just imagine the good things you'll hear!

Nancy Kaczrowski
Luverne, MN

LOYALTY

PERSEVERANCE

Wiggling With Character

Keep a visible reminder of classroom character goals with this year-round display. You will need a large construction-paper circle for each month of the school year, plus one more. For each month choose one value on which to focus; then write the selected values near the tops of the individual circles. Decorate the remaining cutout to resemble the face of a caterpillar. Mount the circles in sequential order on a classroom wall. Be sure the resulting character caterpillar is easily accessible. Each month introduce the selected value, and discuss with your students what the value means and different ways that it can be demonstrated. Label the corresponding caterpillar segment accordingly. Then challenge students to display the featured character trait throughout the month. To reinforce your students' efforts, place a Gummy caterpillar (worm) in a clear container on your desk each time you observe a student displaying the featured value. When you have a class supply, distribute the candies to the students; then start another collection. Throughout the year periodically review the character goals of past months. You can count on plenty of positive growth when you use this approach to character education!

Kristi Gullett—Gr. 2
Peoria Christian School
Peoria, IL

Respect Honesty Fairness

BUILDING CHARACTER
WITH...HONESTY!

Instill the virtue of integrity by teaching the importance of honesty. Use these activities to encourage youngsters to make conscientious and trustworthy decisions.

ideas by Darcy Brown

HONESTY

WHAT WOULD YOU DO?

Inspire your youngsters to make honest and truthful decisions with this notable idea! In advance write a number of decision-making situations on index cards. Place the cards in an empty container. To begin the lesson, have students talk about times they have been in situations that tested their honesty. Then have a child draw a card from the container and read it aloud. Ask youngsters to describe what they would do in this situation and explain why. Encourage discussion among the students. When appropriate have another child draw a card. Repeat the process until all of the cards have been discussed. For added fun invite small groups of students to act out some of the situations.

Your friend asks you to do his homework for him.

You cheat on a test.

HONESTY

HONESTY ACROSTIC POEMS

Help youngsters further investigate honesty when they create these awesome acrostic poems. As your students brainstorm ideas about the importance of being honest, list their ideas on chart paper. Next have each child use capital letters to write the word "honesty" down the left side of a sheet of drawing paper. Instruct students to refer to the chart as they write a descriptive word or phrase that begins with each letter of the word. Allow time for students to decorate their work. If desired mount the completed poems on larger sheets of construction paper. Then spread the word about honesty by displaying the projects around the room.

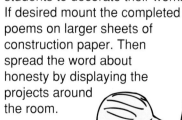

Jocelyn

Honorable
Others trust you
Never lie
Everyone is fair
Say nice things
Tell the truth
You are honest

AS HONEST AS GEORGE WASHINGTON!

Use the famous legend of George Washington and the cherry tree to talk about the importance of telling the truth. Conclude the discussion with this "cherry-ful" activity that reinforces the values of honesty and truthfulness. Provide each student with a white construction-paper copy of the patterns on page 10, a six-inch green pipe cleaner, and a six-inch square of writing paper. Students will also need pencils, scissors, crayons, and access to clear tape and a stapler.

To make a cherry project like the one pictured, a child colors and cuts out her patterns. Next she traces the cherry cutout onto her writing paper. Inside the resulting outline, she completes the sentence starter. Then she cuts out the shape, aligns her colored cherry atop the resulting cutout, and staples the shapes together near the top left edge. To complete her project, the student tapes her leaf cutout near one end of her pipe cleaner and then tapes the resulting stem to the back of her project. Mount the completed cherries on a large paper tree with the title "As Honest As George Washington!"

HONESTY

You should always tell the truth because...

...one's ...Not telling the truth could ma him cry.

FANTASTIC FABLES

Fables are a great way to reinforce students' understanding of good character! Each day read aloud a fable, and discuss the lesson or moral of the story. After youngsters have heard a number of fables, challenge them to write and illustrate original fables that reinforce the importance of honesty. Remind students that the character(s) in their stories should learn a lesson about truthfulness. If desired ask each student to write a moral at the end of his fable that relates to the honesty lesson that he described. Invite stud-ents to share their creations with the rest of the class. Then collect the students' fables and staple them between two construction-paper covers. Add a title such as "Fantastic Fables," a class byline, and desired decorations to the front cover.

Kimberly Hofstetter—Substitute Teacher
Oakland County School District
Bloomfield Hills, MI

A PLEDGE TO BE HONEST

As a culminating activity, have youngsters make a pledge of honesty. Give students copies of the honesty pledge on page 10. Sing the pledge (to the tune of "Sailing, Sailing") or read it aloud as your class follows along. Talk with students about what the pledge means; then ask each child to sign his name and write the date on the lines. If desired have students mount their pledges on slightly larger sheets of construction paper. Challenge youngsters to memorize the pledge, then sing or recite it to others. No doubt your youngsters will perform the pledge with pride!

PLENTIFUL POTS

Use this literature connection to help your young-sters recognize the importance of telling the truth. In the story *The Empty Pot* by Demi (Henry Holt And Company, Inc.; 1990), Ping learns a valuable lesson about honesty and perseverance. After sharing the story with your class, invite students to talk about how Ping's courage and honesty helped him become the emperor of China. Then have your youngsters create these unique reminders to commemorate Ping's accomplishment. Provide each student with a small Styrofoam® cup (with drainage holes punched in the bottom), soil, water, and a choice of flower seeds. Have youngsters use the materials to plant seeds in honor of Ping. Put the seed cups on a tray or cookie sheet and place them in a sunny location in your classroom. Memories of Ping's courage will live on as students care for their seeds.

TRULY TRUTHFUL TALES!

Bolster honest behaviors with these one-of-a-kind stories:

To Tell The Truth
Written by Patti Farmer & Illustrated by Stephen Taylor
Stoddart Kids, 1997

Honest Tulio
Written & Illustrated by John Himmelman
BridgeWater Books, 1997

Believing Sophie
Written by Hazel Hutchins
Illustrated by Dorothy Donohue
Albert Whitman & Company, 1995

Mary Marony And The Chocolate Surprise
Written by Suzy Kline
Illustrated by Blanche Sims
G. P. Putnam's Sons, 1995

Zack's Tall Tale
Adapted by Shelagh Canning
Illustrated by Davis Henry
Aladdin Paperbacks, 1996

King Bob's New Clothes
Written by Dom DeLuise
Illustrated by Christopher Santoro
Simon & Schuster Books For Young Readers, 1996

Patterns And Honesty Pledge

Use the patterns with "As Honest As George Washington!" on page 8.

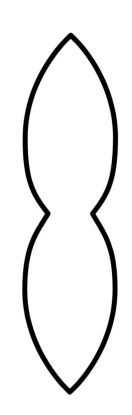

Use the pledge with "A Pledge To Be Honest" on page 9.

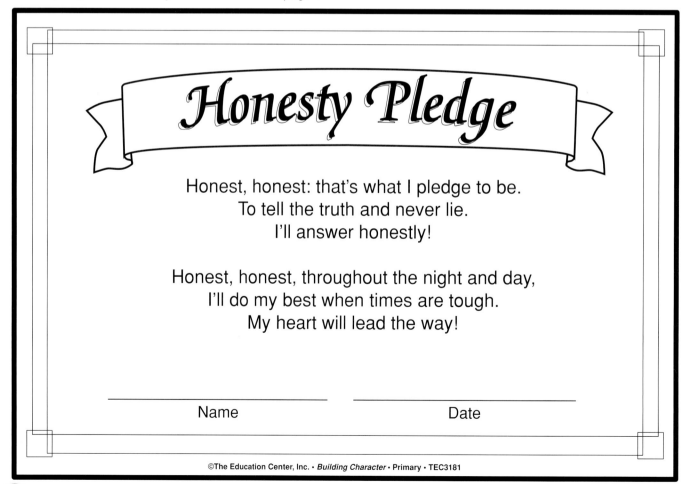

Honesty Pledge

Honest, honest: that's what I pledge to be.
To tell the truth and never lie.
I'll answer honestly!

Honest, honest, throughout the night and day,
I'll do my best when times are tough.
My heart will lead the way!

_____   _____
Name   Date

BUILDING CHARACTER
WITH...CITIZENSHIP

Opportunities for being a good citizen are everywhere—in the classroom, on the playground, at home, and in the community. Use these character-building activities to foster an understanding of citizenship and to promote its importance in our country and in our world.

ideas contributed by Darcy Brown

C I T I Z E N S H I P

Who's A Citizen?

Begin your study of citizenship by informing students that a *citizen* is a member of a special community or group of people. Explain that a person can be a citizen of a very large community like the United States Of America and a person can also be a citizen of much smaller communities like a classroom, a neighborhood, and a city. Inform students that to become a citizen, special requirements must be fulfilled. For example, a classroom citizen must be enrolled in school, attend class regularly, and follow the established rules. Emphasize that being a citizen is a privilege and responsibilities come with this privilege. Then ask students to name the responsibilities that they have as classroom citizens. Wrap up the discussion by giving each student a signed and dated copy of the Classroom Citizen Certificate on page 13. Invite each child to color his certificate; then, if desired, tape each child's certificate to his desktop as a visual reminder of his important classroom role.

Hooray For You

You Are A Valued Citizen In Our Classroom!

Ms. James
Teacher's Signature
6/12/2000
Date

Citizenship Journals

Heighten your students' awareness of classroom citizenship with this daily writing activity. Each child needs a blank writing journal like the one shown. Ask each student to describe in his journal examples of admirable classroom citizenship or citizen behavior. Clarify that students may write about behaviors they observe in other classroom citizens or describe their own acts of good citizenship. After several days of journal writing, divide students into small groups and ask each group member to take a turn reading aloud his favorite journal entry to date. Repeat the group activity as often as desired, varying the groups each time. What a great way to promote citizenship!

My Citizenship Journal Jasmine

Mrs. Weiss
I never litter, I obey the traffic laws, and my family donates gifts to the senior center.

In The Community

Expand your students' understanding of citizens and citizenship in the community by reading aloud Jane Cowen-Fletcher's book *It Takes A Village* (Scholastic Inc., 1994). In this book the members of a close-knit village assist a young girl with her baby-sitting duties. At the conclusion of the story, ask students to recall how different community members help the young girl, and have them speculate why the citizens respond as they do. Remind students that in addition to being classroom citizens, they are also citizens of their local community. Lead students to understand that good citizenship in the local community is fostered in the same manner that it is in the classroom—by being responsible, helpful, compassionate, and so on.

Create a colorful display of community citizenship with this homework activity. Send each child home with a one-foot length of colorful bulletin-board paper. In a parent letter, ask that the child and family members and/or friends trace the shapes of their hands on the paper. Ask that each person cut out and sign his shape, then program it with examples of how he contributes to the well-being of the local community. When the hand cutouts are returned, use them to create a colorful border for a bulletin board titled "Look How We Lend A Hand In Our Community!" To complete the display, have each child illustrate how he or his family lend a hand; then mount the illustrations on the display.

Proud To Be An American

Students may be surprised to discover that not everyone in the United States becomes a citizen in the same way. Many people are born as U.S. citizens, but those who are not must apply and qualify for citizenship. Give students a rare look into the latter process by reading aloud *A Very Important Day* by Maggie Rugg Herold (Morrow Junior Books, 1995). This beautifully illustrated picture book briefly chronicles 12 different families—each from a different country—that make their way to downtown New York City (in a snowstorm) to be sworn in as citizens of the United States. The nervous excitement that is generated by this very special occasion is contagious. As an added bonus, the author has included background information about the citizenship process.

For a fun follow-up, enlist your students' help in locating on a world map each of the 12 countries represented in the book. Then invite students to discuss the things that make them proudest to be U.S. citizens.

A Celebration Of Citizenship

Culminate your study of citizenship with a celebration! Encourage students to invite their parents to your classroom festivities. The guests can view the students' star-spangled projects, read excerpts from their children's citizenship journals, and marvel over the helping-hands display to which they contributed. Plan to serve a healthy and patriotic snack of blueberries, sliced strawberries, and banana wheels. Then conclude the affair with a presentation of citizenship awards. To make an award for each student, program, decorate, and cut out a construction-paper copy of the ribbon pattern on page 13. Students will feel especially honored to be recognized for their citizenship efforts in the presence of their guests. And they'll no doubt be motivated to carry on the good-citizen habits that they have formed during your study.

Karen Smith—Gr. 1
Pine Lane Elementary Homeschool
Pace, FL

Super Citizen

Michele

Student Name

is recognized for

being an exellent listener, a helpful friend , and a great sport.

CITIZENSHIP

Star-Spangled Citizens

Get to the heart of citizenship with this patriotic project. To begin, each student uses templates to trace a seven-inch heart shape onto both blank and lined white paper, a nine-inch heart onto blue paper, and eight or more star shapes onto red paper. Then he cuts out the shapes. On the lined white heart the student describes why he is proud to be a citizen. On the blank white heart he illustrates himself and writes his name. He programs each red star with a good-citizen behavior that he practices. To assemble his project, he glues each smaller heart to a different side of the blue heart. Then he glues the stars around the outer edges of his project in a desired fashion. To prepare the project for hanging, the student hole-punches the top of the project, threads a length of monofilament line through the hole, and securely ties the ends of the line.

Continuous Five-Star Citizenship

Continue encouraging good-citizen behaviors with this weekly activity! Use a permanent marker to personalize a resealable plastic bag for every student. Then, each Monday, place five star cutouts in every bag and distribute the bags among the students. Make sure that no student receives his own bag or a bag that he has already received. Then, during the week, ask each student to quietly observe the student whose bag he has and on each star cutout to write a brief note of praise for a different good-citizen behavior that he observes. For a star-studded end-of-the-week finale, have each student return the bag of citizenship compliments to its owner. Ask the students to remove the stars from their bags, read them, and carry them home to share with their families. Then collect the plastic bags for use the following week.

Pattern And Certificate

Use the certificate with "Who's A Citizen?" on page 11.

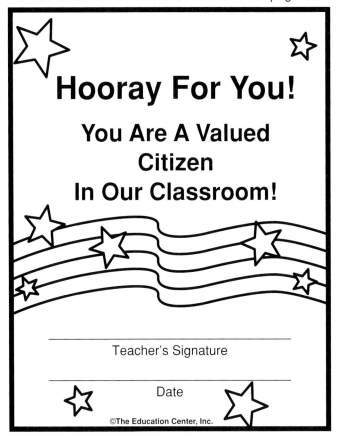

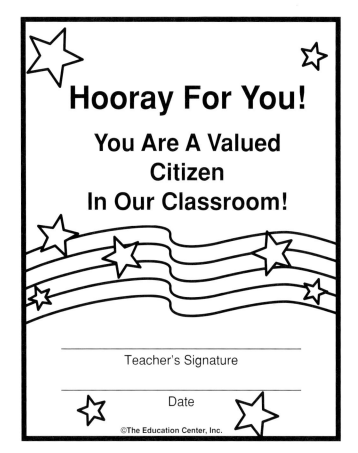

Use the ribbon pattern with "A Celebration Of Citizenship" on page 12.

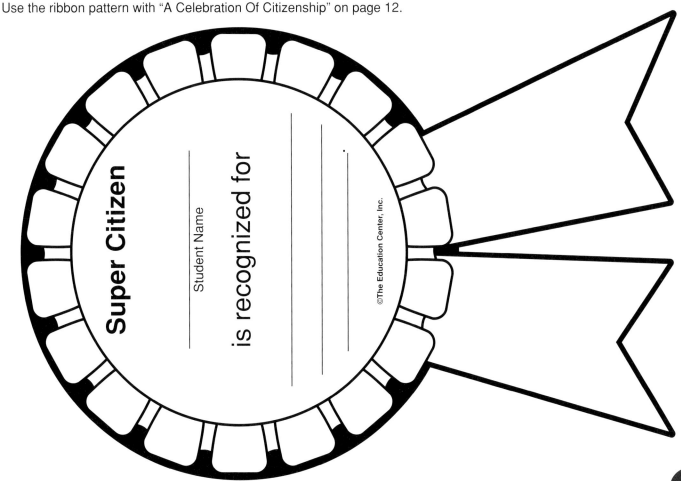

BUILDING CHARACTER
WITH...RESPECT!

Encourage respect among your students with this unique collection of learning activities. You'll be reinforcing positive behaviors and your youngsters will soon see respect as a valued trait in your classroom.

ideas by Darcy Brown

R E S P E C T

Respect is following the rules.

Respectful Reminders

Introduce the meaning of *respect* with these good-as-gold reminders. Begin by asking students to discuss the Golden Rule: *Treat others the way you would like to be treated.* Tell students that when they follow the Golden Rule, they are being respectful and considerate of others and themselves. Next have students name ways they show respect. Then have each youngster make a badge to remind himself (and others) of respectful behaviors. To make a badge, have each child write one way to show respect on a four-inch tagboard circle. Next have him use glue and gold glitter to decorate his badge. When the glue is dry, have the student tape a large safety pin to the back of his badge. Invite your youngsters to wear their badges as respectful reminders throughout your unit of study.

Who's Respectful?

Here's an ideal way to help students understand that showing respect is the first step towards practicing it. Tell your students they can show respect by using good manners. Then read aloud your favorite book about manners. One excellent choice is *Perfect Pigs* by Marc Brown and Stephen Krensky (Little, Brown And Company; 1983). The book's simple text and colorful pictures portray a wide variety of respectful behaviors. Next invite each student to make a flip booklet that shows how she uses good manners. To make a booklet, instruct each youngster to stack two 8 1/2" x 11" sheets of white paper and hold the pages vertically in front of her. Have her slide the top sheet upward approximately one inch. Next direct the youngster to fold the papers forward to create four graduated pages (see the illustration). Have her write the title "Who's Respectful? [Child's name] Is!" and her name on the cover. Then, on the pages, have the youngster write and illustrate how she exhibits good manners at home, at school, and in public. Your students will be flipping over respectful behaviors!

R E S P E C T

Portraits Of Respect

Promote student dignity and self-respect with one-of-a-kind portraits! Explain to your students that when they have a good attitude, make good decisions, and always do their best, they are showing self-respect. Challenge each youngster to name one way she shows self-respect. Then foster self-respect in your students when you invite them to make portraits of themselves. To make a portrait, have each youngster trace a large oval template on a 9" x 12" sheet of drawing paper. Then have her draw a portrait of herself inside the oval. Instruct her to cut out the oval and glue it to a 9" x 12" sheet of construction paper. Next have the student write about self-respect on a sheet of writing paper; then instruct her to attach her sentences to the bottom of her portrait. Have each youngster share her portrait and sentences with her classmates. Display the portraits around the room to remind your students that self-respect begins with them.

14

I am a good listener.

I follow the rules.

Respecting Differences

Convey to your students that respect means treating others the way they would want to be treated—regardless of their differences. To begin, have each youngster name something he likes. Then ask students if they all had the same response. Explain that sometimes people tend to like different things, yet they should all be treated with the same respect. Then ask students to name other ways they may be different from one another. (For instance, students may have different cultural backgrounds, abilities, and appearances.) Next have your students work together to create a mural that honors the differences among people. First have each student cut pictures from catalogs, magazines, and store circulars of different people participating in a variety of activities. Then have the students glue their pictures to a large sheet of bulletin-board paper. Mount the mural under the heading "We Respect Each Other's Differences." What a great way for students to learn to respect one another!

Pledge Of Respect

Wrap up your study of respect by having youngsters make a pledge to respect themselves and each other. Review the different aspects of respect. Copy the pledge shown onto white paper and duplicate one for each student. Read the pledge aloud as your class follows along. Then have students talk about what the pledge means. Next challenge each student to memorize the pledge. If desired, expand the value of respect by having youngsters recite the pledge as part of your morning routine.

Karyn McCroskey—Gr. 2
Pleasant Hope Elementary
Pleasant Hope, MO

Pledge Of Respect
I am a smart, special, and valuable person.
I respect myself and I respect others.
My words and actions are kind and honest.
I accept only my best in all that I do.
I am PROUD TO BE ME!

Two Thumbs-Up!

Your youngsters will give two thumbs-up as they learn about respectful and disrespectful behaviors. As a review, have your students name respectful and disrespectful behaviors; then ask them to describe the possible outcomes of each one. Next read aloud a type of behavior. Have each student display two thumbs-up if the behavior is respectful or two thumbs-down if the behavior is disrespectful. Continue in the same manner until each student has an understanding of respectful and disrespectful behaviors. Extend the lesson by presenting each youngster with a "Thumbs-Up" reward (see illustration) when you observe him displaying a respectful behavior.

Josh
student's name
deserves a thumbs-up for helping Ashley finish her work.

Books About Respect

Foster respect in your students when you share these delightful stories.

How To Lose All Your Friends
Written & Illustrated by Nancy Carlson
Viking Penguin, 1997

Jamaica's Find
Written by Juanita Havill
Illustrated by Anne Sibley O'Brien
Houghton Mifflin Company, 1986

Make Someone Smile And 40 More Ways To Be A Peaceful Person
Written by Judy Lalli
Photographed by Douglas L. Mason-Fry
Free Spirit Publishing Inc., 1996

Mufaro's Beautiful Daughters
Written & Illustrated by John Steptoe
Lothrop, Lee & Shepherd Books; 1987

The Patchwork Quilt
Written by Valerie Flournoy
Illustrated by Jerry Pinkney
Dial Books For Young Readers, 1985

The Wednesday Surprise
Written by Eve Bunting
Illustrated by Donald Carrick
Houghton Mifflin Company, 1989

Marvelous Me!

Demonstrate that being "me" is easy with this collection of upbeat activities and reproducibles.

ideas contributed by Janice Bradley, Chris Christensen, and Lucia Kemp Henry

Star Quality

Invite your youngsters' true colors to shine through as they sing this song to the tune of "Twinkle, Twinkle, Little Star." Everyone *is* a star!

There's No One Like Me!

There's no one who's quite like me.
No one knows just how to be
Me when I am mad or sad,
Me when I am very glad.
There's no one who's quite like me.
I am proud that me is me!

Personal Treasures

You can count on this take-home tote being a total success! Using fabric or puff paints, label a canvas tote bag "Totally Terrific Me!" In a parent note explain that each child is being given the opportunity to take the tote bag home overnight. Ask that the parent provide assistance as his child fills the bag with items and pictures that represent his family and his special interests. Before each student takes the tote bag home, tuck a personalized copy of the parent note inside.

The following day provide time for the special student to share his treasures with his classmates. When the youngster is finished, take a snapshot of him with his special belongings. Then help the student place his treasures in a disposable bag for the trip home. Display the snapshots in a special "Me" photo album.

Friendship Chain

Build self-esteem and friendship link by link with a friendship chain. To introduce the activity, ask each student to label a construction paper strip with a nice comment that a classmate or a peer recently shared with him. Invite students to share their written comments; then, working cooperatively, have students create a friendship chain by looping and gluing their strips together. Display the chain in the classroom. Keep a supply of construction paper strips on hand and invite youngsters to continue adding strips to the class friendship chain. As the friendship chain grows, so will your youngsters' self-esteem.

Just Be Yourself

A lovable lion learns a lion-sized lesson in Don Freeman's delightful book entitled *Dandelion* (The Viking Press). A fancy party invitation prompts a lion to seek superficial grandness through a new wardrobe and hairstyle. It's only after a stormy experience that the lion understands the importance of being himself.

After hearing the story, have youngsters make these "No 'Lion'!" booklets. To make a booklet, color and cut out a construction paper copy of the pattern on page 18. Using an X-acto knife, cut along the dotted lines. Slide one end of a 4" x 18" strip of bulletin board paper under the lion's paws; then glue the paper to the pattern as indicated. Working from the mounted end of the paper, fold the strip accordion-style. Tuck the resulting booklet pages under the lion's paws. Entitle the booklet "No 'Lion'! I'm Proud To Be Me"; then decorate and personalize the cover as desired.

Before having each youngster complete his booklet pages, write several page starters, such as "I feel happy when…" or "The thing I like best about me is…," on the board. Instruct students to copy a different starter onto each booklet page, finish it, and add an illustration. Now that's something to roar about!

My World

Beware! These unique publications might have the media knocking at your classroom door! To begin, have each student draw and color a self-portrait on a 5 1/2" x 8 1/2" sheet of paper. Then have him fold a sheet of 9" x 12" construction paper in half to make a folder and glue his drawing on the cover. Next have the student attach letter cutouts spelling "MY WORLD" and add desired cover copy. Staple several blank pages between each youngster's resulting magazine cover.

Set aside time each day for youngsters to write and illustrate articles in their personal publications. Encourage youngsters to write on topics such as qualities that make them unique, favorite hobbies, and special people in their lives. When the projects are completed, display them for others to read and enjoy. For a unique display, place the magazines in a cardboard greeting card holder. Read all about us!

Operation M.E.

Students piece together the identities of their classmates by reconstructing these student-made puzzles. Duplicate the puzzle pattern (page 19) on white construction paper. Give each youngster an envelope and a copy of the puzzle. Instruct each youngster to draw a self-portrait on his envelope; then have youngsters set the envelopes aside. Next have each student fill in his puzzle pieces by following the directions. When a student has completed his puzzle, have him cut on the lines and place each of his puzzle pieces inside his illustrated envelope. Remind youngsters that their names should not be on any of the work they have just completed.

When all of the envelopes have been gathered, randomly redistribute them. Have each student reconstruct the puzzle he's been given, read the clues, look at the portrait on the envelope, and guess the identity of the puzzle's owner. Whose identity is lurking in that envelope?

Chalking Up Self-Esteem

Thrill your youngsters with this daylong chalkboard activity. To introduce the activity, sign your name on a blank chalkboard and draw a picture of something that makes you feel special about yourself. After explaining what you have just done, invite each of your youngsters to do the same. For a minimal amount of confusion, assign each student a number; then have students visit the chalkboard in numerical order. For a colorful display, allow your youngsters to use colored chalk. When all of your youngsters have signed the chalkboard and completed their drawings, invite each student to tell his classmates about his drawing. This is one time you won't want to erase your chalkboard for several days!

Me Or You Game

Here's a fun game that teaches children to appreciate themselves and others. Label each of five cards ME. Then label each of five additional cards YOU. Place the labeled cards in a decorated container. To play, have students sit in a circle. Pass the container to the first student. If he draws a ME card, the student must say something nice about himself. If he draws a YOU card, he must say something nice about the person to his left. Be sure that each student returns his card to the container before he passes it on to the next person. Continue play until each child has had a turn. Be sure to take a turn yourself!

Booklet Pattern

Use with "Just Be Yourself"
on page 16.

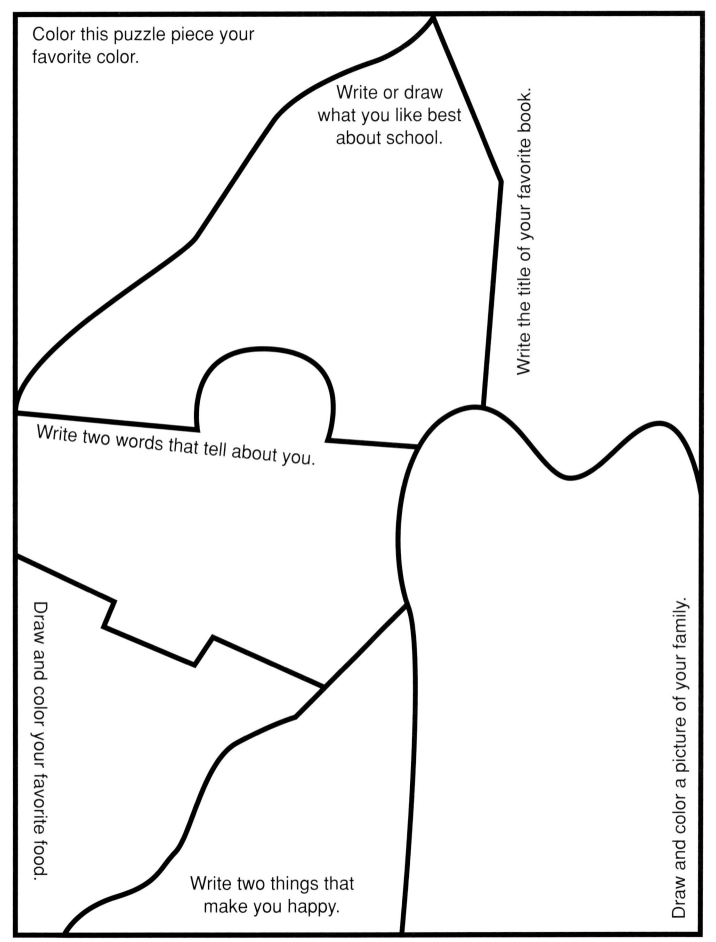

Color this puzzle piece your favorite color.

Write or draw what you like best about school.

Write the title of your favorite book.

Write two words that tell about you.

Draw and color your favorite food.

Write two things that make you happy.

Draw and color a picture of your family.

Note To Teacher: Use with "Operation M.E." on page 17.

Positive Role Models

The challenges that children face today are plentiful. Developing and nurturing self-respect are key to a child's success. Children can also benefit from the influences of positive role models. Use the following activities to help students identify positive role models and understand what they can learn from these people and their experiences.

Researching Positive Role Models

Ask your youngsters what the phrase "positive role model" means to them. After students have shared their ideas, explain the following homework assignment. Instruct each student to interview one adult to learn about a role model that the adult had as a child and why this role model was chosen. Compile the students' interview information on a class chart and evaluate the information together as a class. Ask questions such as "How many role models were family members? Or people in the neighborhood or community? Or celebrities? What were the most frequent reasons for choosing a role model?" In conclusion, invite students to provide additional comments about what the phrase "positive role model" means to them.

Traits Of Role Models

What traits should a positive role model have? Pose this question to the class and list your students' answers on chart paper. Invite discussion and debate about the traits listed; then have each student list what he considers to be the five most important traits. Suggest that students keep their lists for later use.

Identifying Role Models

Whom does a person choose for a role model? Many students will respond that their role models are family members. Others may identify positive role models at school or in their neighborhoods or community. And of course there are plenty of famous folks that children hold in high regard.

In order for a role model to be influential, a youngster must recognize the role model's positive traits. To provide students with practice in this area, have each youngster complete a copy of page 21. This valuable exercise requires a student to evaluate the person he has chosen as a role model. Suggest that each student compare his completed activity to his list of the top five role-model traits (see "Traits Of Role Models"). Are they similar? Provide time for interested students to share their work.

Follow Your Dreams

Positive role models reinforce the importance of courage and determination. This ongoing booklet project encourages students to follow their dreams. To make a booklet, personalize and cut out a copy of the cloud pattern on page 22; then glue it to the front of a folded 9" x 12" sheet of construction paper. If desired, use a silver glitter or paint pen to create a silver lining inside the cloud shape. Then staple a supply of blank booklet pages (page 22) inside this booklet cover. A student completes a booklet page for each of his role models. Any remaining booklet pages can be completed as future role models are discovered.

A Special Person
Write the name of your role model below.

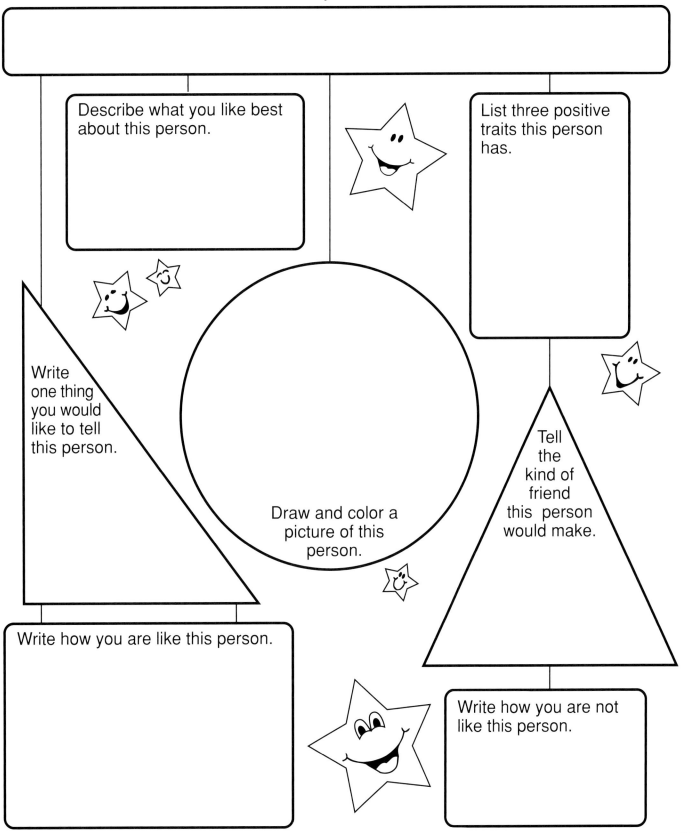

Describe what you like best about this person.

List three positive traits this person has.

Write one thing you would like to tell this person.

Draw and color a picture of this person.

Tell the kind of friend this person would make.

Write how you are like this person.

Write how you are not like this person.

Note To Teacher: Use with "Identifying Role Models" on page 20.

I Plan To Follow My Dreams

by

_____

©The Education Center, Inc. • *Building Character* • Primary • TEC3181

	This person is my role model
	because_____
	_____
	_____
	_____.
	_____will inspire me to follow
	He/She
Name: _____	my dreams because_____
Description: _____	
_____	_____.

©The Education Center, Inc. • *Building Character* • Primary • TEC3181

Note To Teacher: Use the pattern and booklet page with "Follow Your Dreams" on page 20.

Catchy Compliments

Recognize and encourage your youngsters' outstanding efforts with this collection of complimentary kudos. Use the following suggestions to get your youngsters hooked on positive behaviors and study habits:

Say 'Em Out Loud—Tell a youngster how proud you are of his work or terrific behavior.

Write 'Em Down—Add variety to the comments that you write on students' work.

Put 'Em On Display—Use the phrases as bulletin-board titles. Spotlight students' work on the resulting displays.

Hand 'Em Out—Reproduce the complimentary cards on page 24 on colorful construction paper. Cut the cards apart; then hand them out to deserving students. You may wish to provide a special reward for each student who earns a predetermined number of cards.

Judy Coffman—Gr. 3, Heritage Elementary, Keller, TX

- I like the way you think of others.
- As a leader, you are ahead of the pack.
- When it comes to being a good listener—you are all ears!
- It's how you play the game that makes you a winner!
- Your ideas shine brighter than the sun!
- You are really organized!
- I like the way you stay on track.
- The way you pitch in, you'll never strike out!
- You're a real team player! Thanks for participating.
- Three cheers for you!
- I like the way you encourage your classmates.
- How could I forget someone who always remembers homework!
- You've been as busy as a bee! Thanks for staying on task.
- If good work were gold, you'd be a millionaire!
- Are you marvelous in math? Let me count the ways!
- Touchdown! Your outstanding effort made the difference.
- Your cheerfulness is contagious!
- Thanks for your thoughtfulness.

Note To Teacher: Use with "Catchy Compliments" on page 23.

Follow The Yellow Brick Road

Join Dorothy and her friends on a journey down the yellow brick road to success. Reaching inside themselves to find knowledge, courage, and feelings of love and security, students can heighten their self-awareness and find that they have the ability to make their dreams come true. Whether you make the journey as a class, or plan a schoolwide extravaganza, there's no turning back!

ideas by Linda Regester—Special Education, Garden Plain Elementary
Garden Plain, KS

Pam Crane

Off To Find Success

Working in small groups, have students set the scene for their upcoming journey. Give each of five groups one of the following cutouts to decorate: the wizard's castle, Dorothy and Toto, Scarecrow, Lion, Tin Man. At the top of a large display area, mount a banner bearing the caption "Follow The Yellow Brick Road To Success." At the upper left corner of the display attach the student-decorated castle. Add the remaining cutouts in conjunction with the following activities.

The Yellow Brick Road

The road to success is paved with… yellow bricks! Have each student trim the corners of a yellow construction paper rectangle to create a brick shape. On his cutout, have the student write a dream for the future. Starting at the door of the castle cutout, use the bricks to "pave a road." Extend the road down and across your display in a fashion similar to the yellow brick road shown on the next two pages.

Scarecrow Savvy

The straw-filled Scarecrow yearned for wisdom and knowledge. To help students realize the importance of an education, have small groups of students brainstorm and list reasons why an education is valuable. As a class, discuss the reasons each group listed. Write a compiled list on the chalkboard. On white construction paper, duplicate student copies of the diploma pattern on page 28. Have each student cut out his diploma, then refer to the list to complete the sentence. For a three-dimensional effect, have each student roll the lower edge of his cutout around a pencil, then remove the pencil. Attach a ribbon length to the back of the cutout so it will extend beyond the curl.

Mount the Scarecrow cutout from "Off To Find Success" atop your yellow brick road. Around the Scarecrow, display the diplomas and the caption "Learn As Much As You Can!"

25

Roaring With Courage

Handicapped by his fears, the Cowardly Lion lacked confidence in himself. But when he was faced with the challenge of saving Dorothy from the Wicked Witch of the West, the Lion put all fears aside and displayed exemplary courage. Help students realize that courage takes many forms—courage to be oneself, to overcome peer pressure, and to pursue individual goals. After a discussion about courage, give each student a yellow construction paper copy of the medal pattern on page 28. Have each student cut out his medal and complete the sentence. Then have students embellish their completed awards with foil, ribbon, or glitter.

Mount the Lion cutout from "Off To Find Success" atop your yellow brick road. Display the caption "Discover Your Courage" and the medals nearby.

Homeward Bound

Dorothy dreamed of a wonderful land over the rainbow, but when she traveled to this mysterious land, she realized how much the love and support of her family really meant to her. Discuss the importance of family rules and showing support for each family member. Then have small groups of students dramatize familiar family situations such as parents being "too strict," children not doing their chores, or siblings arguing. After each scene is dramatized, have students discuss the situation and offer possible solutions. On light-colored construction paper, duplicate student copies of the house pattern on page 28. Have each child cut out a pattern, complete the sentence, and illustrate himself looking out the window.

Mount the Dorothy and Toto cutout from "Off To Find Success" atop your yellow brick road. Close by, display the house cutouts and the caption "Be Thankful For Your Family."

Heartfelt Sentiments

Lack of a heart did not keep the tenderhearted Tin Man from expressing his feelings and concerns for others. Lead students in a discussion about feelings. Ask them how they can show others they care. Find out how helping others makes them feel. On pink construction paper, duplicate student copies of the heart pattern on page 28. Have each child cut out his copy and complete the sentence. Then have him glue his cutout atop a heart-shaped doily.

Mount the Tin Man cutout from "Off To Find Success" atop the yellow brick road. Display the hearts and the caption "Feel With Your Heart" around the Tin Man.

Education is important to me because it helps me learn to use my talents and learn about the world.
Tyler

It took courage for me to sing a solo at the PTA program last month.
Alex

Smart Choices

To realize their dreams, Dorothy and her friends overcame the forces of the Wicked Witch of the West. Understanding the values of an education, self-esteem, love, and security will help students overcome obstacles blocking their paths to success. Have students brainstorm a list of possible obstacles such as using drugs and alcohol, and poor eating habits. As a follow-up activity, make smart-choice collages. Have each student cut out and mount magazine pictures which represent a healthful lifestyle atop a sheet of construction paper. Entitle the collages "My Choices For Success."

Off To See The Wizard

Residents of the Land of Oz believed the Wizard performed magic. But Dorothy and her friends learned that the wizard's true magic was helping others have faith in themselves. This colorful critical-thinking project will do just that! Trim a nine-inch paper plate to resemble a hot-air balloon; then sponge paint a colorful design onto the bottom of the plate. Vertically cut a Styrofoam cup in half. Along the top edge of one half, punch three evenly spaced holes. Tie one end of an 8-inch length of ribbon through each hole. Glue the cup half atop a sheet of light blue construction paper as shown. When the glue is dry, extend and tape each unattached ribbon length to the paper. Glue the "hot air balloon" top the ribbon ends.

On a five-inch, white construction-paper square, have each student write his wish for the world. On a second square, have him write how he can help make his wish come true. Trim the squares into cloud shapes. Glue the cutouts atop the balloon projects. Dreams can come true!

There's No Place Like...

Click! Click! Click! Create school and community pride with this cooperative learning activity. Throughout the year, have students compile a scrapbook of pictures, newspaper clippings, personal writings, and other memorabilia about their school and community. At the end of the year, place the scrapbook in the school office. Ask that it be shared with visitors and new students the following year. Or produce a video scrapbook. Invite parents and school and community leaders to an end-of-the-year screening. Then place the video in the school library for teachers to check out and view with their students.

Patterns
Use with pages 25 and 26.

diploma

*E*ducation is important to me because
_____
_____
_____
_____
_____
_____
_____

medal

*I*t took courage for me to _____
_____
_____
_____

house

*M*y family is special to me because

heart

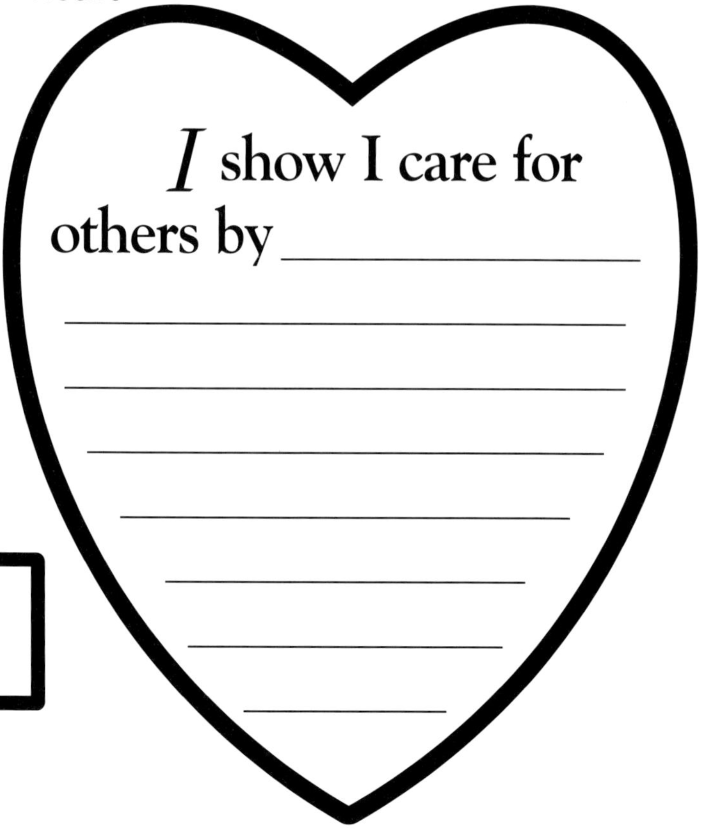

I show I care for others by _____
_____
_____
_____
_____
_____

Another Set of Plans to Build Character

Student Support

This activity encourages students to interact with classmates who have experienced similar events and/or emotions. At least once a week, gather your youngsters together in a comfortable setting and discuss the "current events" of their lives. Promote the sharing of joyful events as well as events that have caused unwanted feelings. Openly discuss each situation that is presented and invite students who have had similar experiences to share helpful advice. If desired, invite special guests such as the school principal or nurse to join your discussions. These weekly sessions help to foster a valuable support system among your students.

Mary Beth Ghoreyeb—Gr. 2, Brewster School, Durham, CT

Kevin

You are nice to everyone.

I like your smile.

You are good at math.

You tell funny jokes.

Creating Sunny Days

Brighten a cloudy day with this self-esteem booster. Ask each student to write his name on a sheet of blank paper, then display the paper on his desktop. Be sure to do the same yourself! Then have each student take his pencil and move from desk to desk, stopping at each one to write a positive comment on each person's paper. For easy management, have students move along a predetermined route. Students will beam with delight when they return to their desks and read the sunny messages that are awaiting them.

Laura Mihalenko—Gr. 2
Truman Elementary School
Parlin, NJ

Incentive Bracelets

Build motivation and self-esteem with incentive bracelets. Keep a stack of paper strips (7" x 1") on your desk. When a student has a good day or does something exceptional, tape a strip around his wrist and add a sticker. Your students will love wearing these bracelets home to show their families.

Betty Ann Morris—Gr. 2
Liestman Elementary
Houston, TX

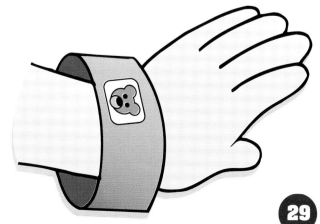

Calling All Helpers

Create an opportunity for students to follow directions and behave responsibly at this helper center. Assign one or two students to the center each day. Provide a list of jobs to complete (such as placing stickers on papers or straightening bookshelves) and needed supplies. Students will take great pride in their classroom contributions.

Lona Richie
Perry County District #32
Perryville, MO

Kindness Counts

Boost your youngsters' self-esteem by spotlighting their kind deeds. To do this, place a supply of paper slips and a large basket (or other appealing container) near your desk. When a student compliments a classmate or receives a compliment from a classmate, he anonymously describes the incident on a slip of paper and places the paper in the basket. On Friday, empty the basket. With your youngsters' help, count the number of kind deeds recorded during the week. Also read aloud a random sampling of the deeds. Return the empty basket to its original location and repeat the activity the following week.

Leigh Anne Newsom—Gr. 3
Greenbrier Intermediate School
Chesapeake, VA

Kevin helped me finish my math.

Sarah sat with me at lunch.

Rich helped me clean up after art.

A Chain Of Thanks

Here's a seasonal center that's certain to stir up thoughts of thankfulness. Each student needs 14 construction paper strips. Label one strip for each of the following letters: *T, H, A, N, K, S.* Label each of six more strips with a thankful thought. Glue the ends of a blank strip together to form the first loop of the chain. Attach the strip labeled *T* to the beginning loop; then attach a strip labeled with a thankful thought to the second loop. Continue in this manner—alternating between the two types of labeled strips—so the word "THANKS" is displayed down one side of the chain. Color and personalize a seasonal cutout; then loop the remaining construction paper strip through the chain, and glue the completed cutouts between its ends. Suspend the completed chains from lengths of yarn or monofilament line for an attractive display.

Sr. Ann Claire Rhoads
Mother Seton School
Emmitsburg, MD

A Banner Of Thanks

Students quickly get into the swing of using good manners with this colorful display. With your youngsters' assistance, create a list of key words that are found in politely stated requests and responses such as "Thank you," "Please," "You're welcome," and "Excuse me." Then have each student copy a different word or phrase from the list onto a large, construction-paper triangle. Attach the triangles to a length of yarn or string; then suspend the resulting "banner of manners" in a highly visible location, such as across the top of your chalkboard.

Gina Parisi—Gr. 2, Demarest School, Bloomfield, NJ

Team Up For The Needy

Anytime is the right time to team up with an upper-elementary class to help the needy. Begin by enlisting students to help plan and man a bake sale. Contact parent volunteers and ask for donations of individually wrapped baked goods. With the proceeds from the sale in hand, chaperone class representatives as they select and purchase nutritious, nonperishable food items at a grocery store. After the students involved have had an opportunity to see the food items that were purchased, donate the food to a local food pantry. This worthwhile project is likely to be an important learning experience for your students since, in working on it, they will have used many academic skills, cooperated with others, and learned something about the merits of helping others.

Susan Bell—Gr. 2
Wedgewood Elementary
St. Charles, MO

Hand over this bulletin board to your students! To create the border have students trace their hands atop sheets of colorful construction paper and cut out the resulting shapes. Then have students draw and color posters showing ways they can work together toward a successful school year. Mount the border, posters, and title as shown. No doubt about it! This display will be a hands-down favorite!

Marge Westrich—Gr. 2, Colby Elementary School, Colby, WI

Reproducible Activities...

CHARACTER BUILDING

from Teacher's Helper® magazine.

How To Use Pages 35–39

1. In preparation for making the booklet, duplicate a construction-paper copy of pages 35, 36, 37, 38, and 39 for each student. Cut pages 35, 36, 37, and 38 along the exterior lines and along the dotted center line.

2. To make the cover of the booklet, begin by tracing each student's hand onto colored construction paper. Have each student cut out her hand shape and glue it to the cover of the booklet (top of page 35). Also have her write her name.

3. On the first booklet page (bottom of page 35), have each student write her age in the box and draw and color the corresponding number of candles on her cake.

4. On the second booklet page (top of page 36), have each student write the name of her favorite color in the box and color the paint puddle to match.

5. On the third booklet page (bottom of page 36), have each student write the name of her favorite book in the box and draw a picture to represent the story on the book cover illustration.

6. On the fourth booklet page (top of page 37), have each student choose a skill that she is good at and write the name of the skill in the box. Then have her draw and color a related picture in the space on the "newspaper."

7. On the fifth booklet page (bottom of page 37), have each student choose a thing, person, or event that makes her happy. Have her write her choice in the box and illustrate it on the present.

8. On the sixth booklet page (top of page 38), have each student write about something that makes her feel scared. Have her draw a picture in the flashlight's beam to accompany her answer.

9. On the seventh booklet page (bottom of page 38), have each child write the number of family members she has. Then have her draw a family portrait.

10. Have each student write her name and use available supplies to decorate page 39 to resemble herself.

11. Stack the booklet pages in order and staple them where indicated to page 39.

All About Me

by

1. Trace your right hand on construction paper.

2. Cut it out.

3. Glue it here.

1

I am ☐ years old.

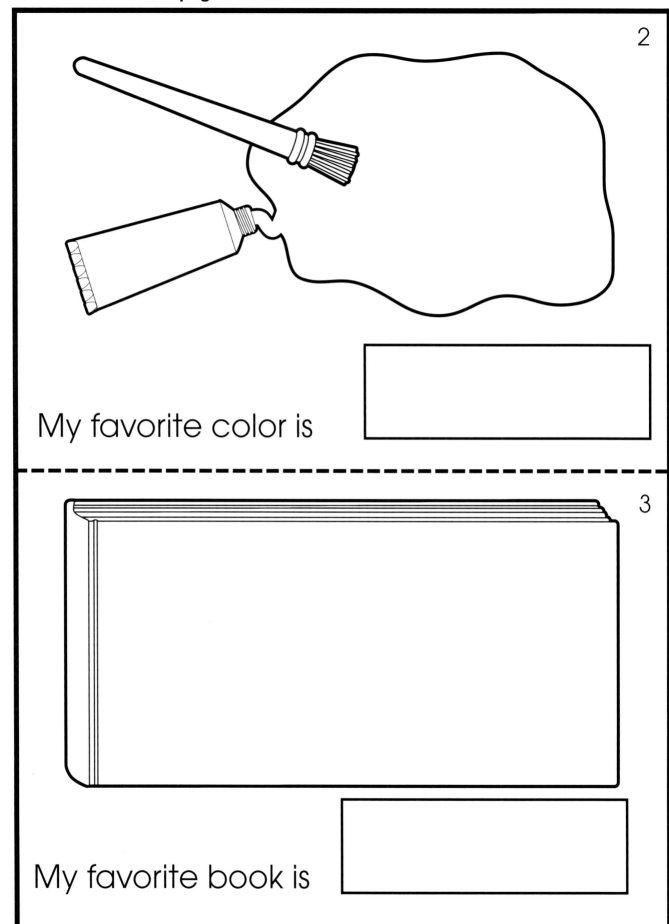

2

My favorite color is

3

My favorite book is

Special News Headlines

4

Read All About It!

You are good
at doing
something
special!

I am good at

5

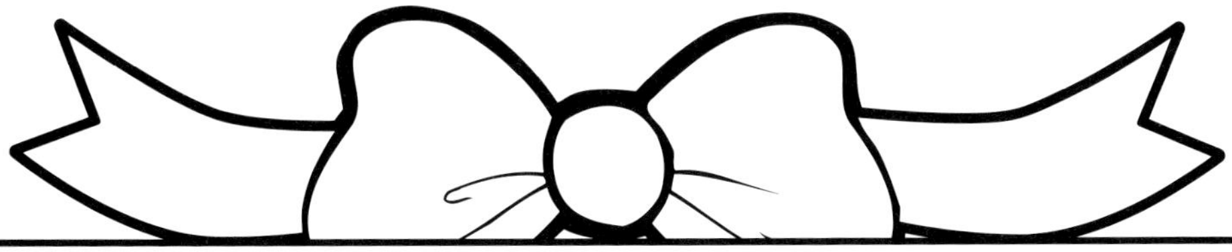

I feel happy about

6

I get scared when

7

My family has ☐ people.

Staple pages here.

is special!

Friendships Mean the World to Me

Materials Needed For Each Student
— copy of page 41 and the booklet pages below
— 7" square of red or pink construction paper
— pencil
— crayons or markers
— scissors
— glue
— access to a stapler

How To Use Pages 40 And 41
1. Engage students in a discussion about *friends* and *friendship.* Lead them to realize that friendships are fostered by *being* a good friend!
2. On the chalkboard write the sentence starter "A friend is someone who…" and a list of student-generated endings.
3. Distribute page 41 and the booklet pages below. Instruct students to complete the five sentence starters on the lines and illustrate their ideas in the hearts.
4. Next have each student color and personalize the booklet cover, title page, and globe pattern on page 41.

How To Assemble The Friendship Booklet
1. Cutting on the heavy outlines, cut out the globe and three large rectangles.
2. Glue the globe cutout to the construction-paper square; then trim the paper to create a narrow border. Set the cutout aside.
3. Using the thin lines as guides, fold each rectangle in half so that the programming remains on the outside.
4. Stack the resulting booklet cover and pages in sequential order. Staple the booklet to the globe pattern as shown on page 41.

Booklet Pages

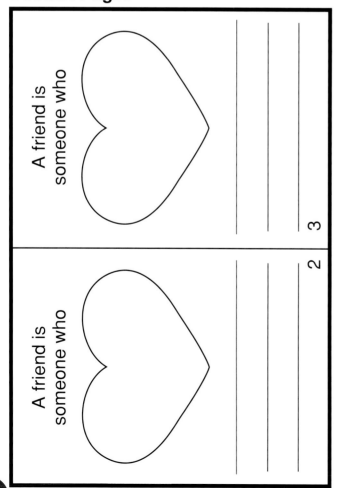

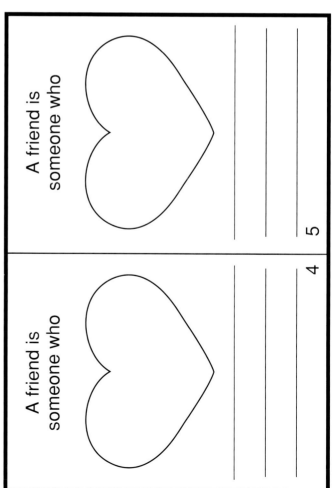

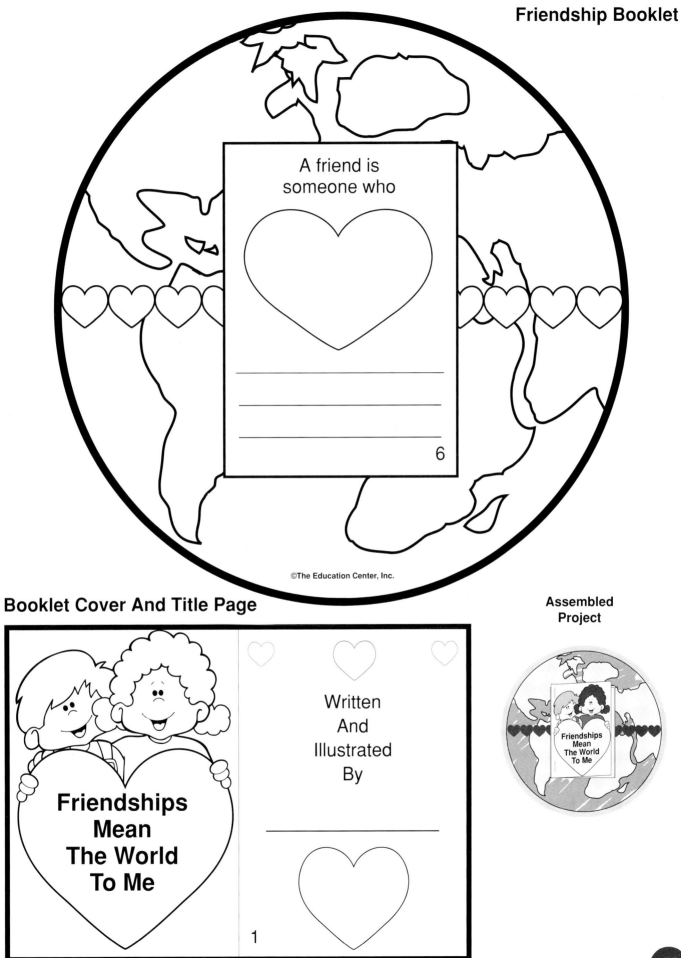

A friend is
someone who

6

©The Education Center, Inc.

Booklet Cover And Title Page

Assembled Project

Friendships Mean The World To Me

Written
And
Illustrated
By

1

Materials Needed

—scissors
—pencils
—crayons
—markers
—yarn (optional)
—colorful construction paper
—stapler
—glue

How To Use Pages 43–48

For each student, duplicate pages 43, 44, 45, 46, and 47 on duplicating paper. Duplicate the cover pattern (on page 48) on white construction paper. Have students cut the booklet pages and cover along the dark lines. Then have students put the booklet pages in numerical order, placing the covers on top. Staple booklets together at the tops. Have students decorate their covers to resemble themselves. Then work through the booklet as a group. When finished, encourage students to share their booklets with friends and family.

I am in _second_ grade.
I write with my _right_ hand.
This is what my thumbprints look like:

My Self-Portrait

left   right

1

I Am Special!

There is no one quite like me.

My full name is _____

_____

but I like to be called _____

I am _____ years old.

I have _____ eyes and

_____ hair.

I am in _____ grade.

I write with my _____

hand.

This is what my thumbprints

look like:

| left | right |

My Self-Portrait

1

I Have People Who Care About Me!

My family and friends are important to me.

This is my family.

These are my friends.

My family is special because _____

My friends are special because _____

2

I Do Many Things Well!

The best thing about me is _____

My best school subject is _____

because _____

I work very hard to _____

When I'm at home, I like to _____

I like to _____ _____ with my friends.

Design an award for yourself!
Write what the award is for.
Color and decorate your award.

3

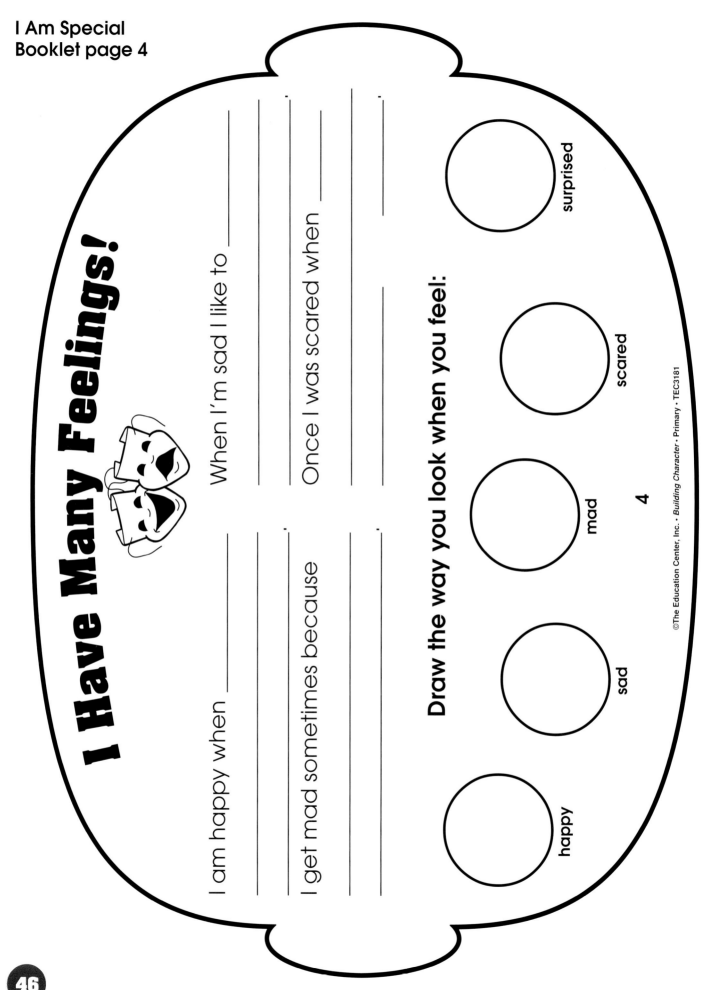

I Have Many Feelings!

I am happy when _____

When I'm sad I like to _____

I get mad sometimes because _____

Once I was scared when _____

Draw the way you look when you feel:

happy

sad

mad

scared

surprised

4

I Have Plans For The Future!

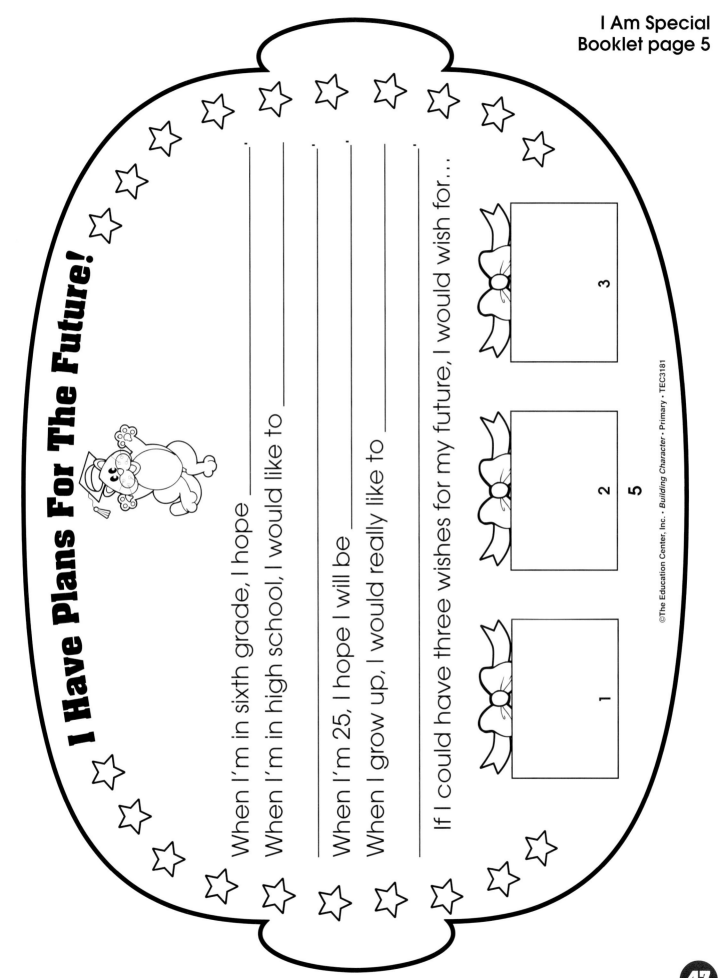

When I'm in sixth grade, I hope _____

When I'm in high school, I would like to _____

When I'm 25, I hope I will be _____

When I grow up, I would really like to _____

If I could have three wishes for my future, I would wish for...

| 1 | 2 | 3 |

5

©The Education Center, Inc. • *Building Character* • Primary • TEC3181

I Am Special
Booklet cover